Color Poems

Selected by John Foster

First published in the United States of America in 2008 by
dingles & company
P.O. Box 508
Sea Girt, New Jersey 08750

First Printing

Website: www.dingles.com

E-mail: info@dingles.com

Library of Congress Catalog Card No.: 2007907142

ISBN: 978-1-59646-590-9 (library binding)
        978-1-59646-591-6 (paperback)

© Oxford University Press   *10/09*
This U.S. edition of *Color Poems*, originally published in English in 1994 as *Colour Poems*, is published by arrangement with Oxford University Press.

Acknowledgments
The editor and publisher wish to thank the following who have kindly given permission for the use of copyright material:

Pie Corbett for "I Like Colors", originally published as "I Like Colours", © Pie Corbett 1994
Eric Finney for "Mixing Colors", originally published as "Mixing Colours", © Eric Finney 1994
John Foster for "Traffic Lights", © John Foster 1994
Judith Nicholls for "Color Mix", originally published as "Colour Mix", © Judith Nicholls 1994
Charles Thomson for "My Favorite Color", originally published as "My Favourite Colour", © Charles Thomson 1994

Illustrations by
Amelia Rosato; Thelma Lambert; Fiona Dunbar; Caroline Ewen; Lesley Harker; Jon Higham; Karen Donnelly

Printed in China

.ₓ.• dingles&company

I Like Colors

I like blue.
I like the sky
where birds fly high.

I like yellow.
I like the sun
when we have fun.

3

I like green.
I like frogs
as still as logs.

I like black.
I like the dark
when foxes bark.

Pie Corbett

My Favorite Color

My favorite color is red —
red like a mailbox.

I've got red shirts and shoes.
I've got red shorts and socks.

And when I run around,
or when I shout and yell,

my best friend laughs and says
my face is red as well.

Charles Thomson

Mixing Colors

Mix red and blue for purple.
Mix red and white for pink.
Mix red and black and yellow,
and you'll get brown, I think.

Why don't you mix some colors?
Mix two or three or four.
You might just mix a color
No one's ever mixed before.

Eric Finney

Golden Fries

Brown potatoes, white potatoes —
change them if you can.
Turn them into golden fries,
sizzling in the pan.

Anonymous

Color Mix

A ladybug's back
is spotted with black,
though most of it is red.

A tiger's back
is yellow and black,
and so is a tiger's head.

A leopard's back
is yellow and black;
but he has spots instead!

Judith Nicholls

Traffic Lights

Red at the top
says, "You must stop."

Red and yellow between
say, "Get ready for green."

Green below
says, "You can go."

John Foster

Roses Are Red

Roses are red.
Spiders are black.
Don't look now
but there's one on your back!

Anonymous

16

Sounds Poems

Selected by John Foster

First published in the United States of America in 2008 by
dingles & company
P.O. Box 508
Sea Girt, New Jersey 08750

First Printing

Website: www.dingles.com

E-mail: info@dingles.com

Library of Congress Catalog Card No.: 2007907142

ISBN: 978-1-59646-590-9 (library binding)
978-1-59646-591-6 (paperback)

© Oxford University Press
This U.S. edition of *Sounds Poems*, originally published in English in 1995, is published by arrangement with Oxford University Press.

Acknowledgments
The editor and publisher wish to thank the following who have kindly given permission for the use of copyright material:

John Foster for "On Rainy Days", © John Foster 1995
Julie Holder for "Loud and Soft" and "Footsteps", both © Julie Holder 1995
Ian Larmont for "Sounds Like Me", © Ian Larmont 1995
Daphne Lister for "The Echo Bridge", © Daphne Lister 1995
Tony Mitton for "My Big Band", © Tony Mitton 1995
Judith Nicholls for "Can You Hear?", © Judith Nicholls 1995

Illustrations by
Stephanie Strickland; Kay Widdowson; Graham Round; Jane Gedye;
Jan Lewis; Jane Bottomley; Willow

Printed in China

Sounds Like Me

Roar like a lion.
Squeak like a mouse.
Meow like a cat
locked out of a house.

Howl like a wolf.
Buzz like a bee.
Then shout with your own voice,
"Hello! This is me!"

Ian Larmont

My Big Band

"Ting" went the triangle.
"Foo" went the flute.
"Whee" went the whistle.
The horn went "toot."

"Crash" went the cymbal.
"Boom" went the drum.
"Ta-ra" went the trumpet.
"Quiet!" yelled Mom.

Tony Mitton

Loud and Soft

YOU MUST SHOUT
IF I'M FAR AWAY
SO I CAN HEAR
WHAT YOU WANT TO SAY.

22

But if you and I
are near,
you can whisper
and I will hear.

Julie Holder

The Echo Bridge

There's an old bridge
where I sometimes go,
if I stand underneath it
and shout, "Hello!"

"Hello, hello, hello,"
I hear the call.
Yet there's no one else there —
just me, that's all

I roar like a lion,
and one roars back.
I howl like a wolf,
and I hear the whole pack.

I growl like a tiger,
and more growls come.
I feels so scary —
I run back home to Mom.

Daphne Lister

Footsteps

Hiking boots tramp,
rubber boots stamp,
slippers slap,
flip-flops flap,
sneakers squeak
on shiny floors.
Bare feet pad, pad, pad,
like paws.

Julie Holder

Can You Hear?

The wind is a giant's breath.
I can hear him under my door.
He puffs and pants.
He moans and groans.
He whistles across my floor.

Judith Nicholls

On Rainy Days

The rain slaps and taps
against windowpanes.

The rain drops and plops
into puddles in lanes.

The rain giggles and gurgles
as it slurps down drains.

John Foster